SENDING SIGNALS

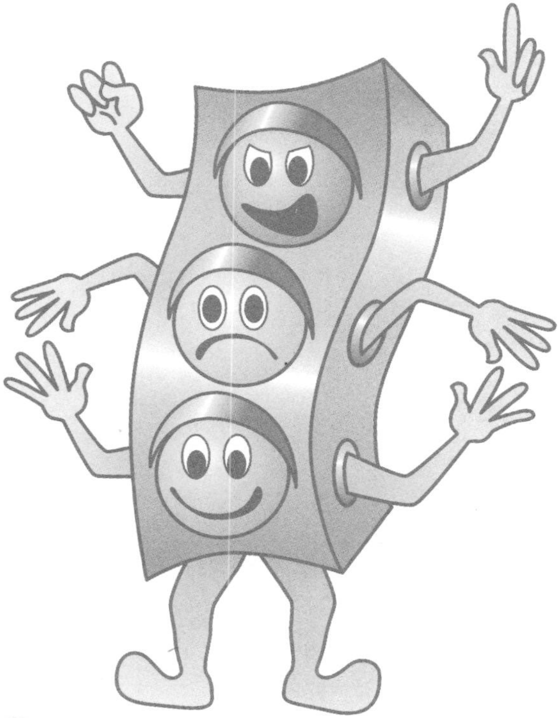

Nancy,
Dream
Live
Love

SENDING SIGNALS

Cruisin' Through Life With Leadership

by Brian Blasko

Finish Line Publishing, Inc.

Published by Finish Line Publishing, Inc.
P.O. Box 3329
Youngstown, OH 44513

ISBN # 978-0-9718630-2-6

Cover Design by:
Jim Valentini
Creative Services

First Edition

Printed in the United States

CITYPRINTING

Printed by City Printing Company, Youngstown, Ohio

 10

D7746   09/08   2M

CONTENTS

Part One .... Introduction

Part Two ....Preparation & Supplies

Part Three .... The Human Race

Part Four ....The Next Day

Part Five ....Today

CHARACTERS

RUDY REDLIGHT

Aggressive / Domineering / Authoritarian

YONNY YELLOWLIGHT

Passive / Indecisive / Tentative

GERTIE GREENLIGHT

Assertive /Proactive /Optimistic

Leadership is a choice ... not a Title!

Whether you're a CEO, supervisor, manager, coach, entrepreneur, or stay at home parent one thing is for sure, leadership moments exist daily.

Sending Signals is an exceptional new book, filled with strategies and tactics for becoming a successful leader. Written in an allegory format, it tells the story of three incredible characters and their quest for freedom. Winning is everything to Rudy, Yonny, and Gertie, but as the story unfolds you'll find that winning is *only* possible when these individuals become a team.

Sit back, relax and enjoy this unforgettable journey into an imaginary world, not too unlike the one you live in today.

To Laura
My journey to happiness, love and
feeling complete starts with You

PART ONE
INTRODUCTION

PART ONE
INTRODUCTION

Once upon a time, in a place not too far away from your home town, there lived a little traffic light. Now, this was not any ordinary traffic light, for you see this traffic signal was very special — it was almost human in fact. The little traffic light was home to three occupants, Rudy Redlight, Yonny Yellowlight, and Gertie Greenlight. They ate, slept, worked and played, just like you and I, but each one had its own unique personality and its own leadership style. Although they lived together within the same yellow metal casing, each one led a separate existence with its own unique goals, visions and dreams. Despite their different personalities and different ways of sending signals, these three traffic lights lived happily together, and they usually managed to get along with one another very well. There was, however, one time a year when Rudy, Yonny and Gertie did not get along so well—and that was during The Human Race.

For the past 75 years, The Human Race has been an annual event involving traffic lights, signals and road signs around the world. Signals and signs of every shape, color and size compete in the international contest that lasts 48 hours or more, over a full weekend. But strangely enough, this Human Race has been one of the best-kept secrets from humans for all those years. It takes place annually without a glitch, right in front of our eyes, but for some reason, we humans have no idea it exists. And that's exactly the way the traffic lights and road signs want it. They feel instinctively that human beings would not be able to cope with talking lights and signs, and chances are they're right!

The Human Race features participants traveling over land, under water and through the air to get to the finish line. The hard work and dedication that goes into winning the race is well worth the effort, because winning this secret race is their only chance for freedom. You see, the winner of the race is granted a very special prize...to become human! It is a little known fact that all traffic lights and road signs want to become human, and our friends Rudy, Yonny and Gertie are no exception. They want nothing more than to receive this great honor, but for some reason, it never happens to them. Every year, winning The Human Race is their goal and their dream, and every year they manage to lose the race, each one in his or her own way.

The Human Race of 1954 was the only time a traffic light ever won the race. That year was special, and that traffic light made it into the history books. To this day, no one actually knows how the traffic light won, but what we do know is that it was a magical moment. The winning light became human, and the other competitors were never seen or heard from again. Legend has it that a journal containing a "secret" winning strategy was kept by the victor. The journal supposedly contained the secret of success for winning The Human Race, but it had never been found, and some of the signs and signals started to doubt its very existence.

In past competitions, Rudy, Yonny and Gertie always argued among themselves. Each of them had their own strategy for winning, but they always wound up working against one another instead of cooperating. This lack of teamwork caused them considerable anguish and led them to defeat, year after year. The problem was that their focus was on being the individual victor; they never thought about combining their leadership styles and skills to win as a team. In fact, during one competition a few years back, Rudy actually sabotaged the race for Yonny and Gertie. Rudy the know-it-all decided he would save his friends the shame and embarrassment of crossing the finish line at the back of the pack, so he set up a fake detour—and his two friends fell for it! They vowed revenge, but for some reason, they could never muster the determination to pay him back with some of his own medicine. In fact, not once did any of these three friends lend a helping hand, or even think about what they could offer each other.

These short-sighted, selfish tactics got them nowhere, of course. Then one day, shortly before that start of the annual Human Race, one of them had a bright idea. Gertie said to her friends, "Hey, what do you think about working together this year? We could combine our different leadership styles and be more successful." Rudy immediately said, "No Way!" He believed that working with the others would only slow him down; he always had to have things his way. He felt their leadership styles would only prevent him from being the boss, which is what he always wanted to be. He wanted things done right, so he wanted things done his way; building consensus and sacrificing for the team was for the birds! His strategy for winning The Human Race was familiar, like the one some humans have for running a business: ONE LEADER / ONE WAY, and that's it!

Yonny didn't say much except, "Oh, I don't know, whatever you two think is best will be all right with me." He wanted to say that working together might be a good idea, but his usual passive, go-along to get-along style was getting the best of him that day.

Gertie quickly responded, "I think that combining forces and blending our leadership tactics would be great for us. We could work together as a team, pool our talents and leadership styles, and maybe win this thing for once. After all, it's the whole stoplight that gets the honors if we win. All of us will benefit!"

But with only a few days to go, time was running

out for a change of race strategy. Gertie realized that she was going to have a hard time convincing her two friends to adopt her bold idea of cooperation and consensus, but she was not ready to give up on them just yet. She was convinced they could be persuaded to make the big step forward: this year things were going to be different, she vowed. This year, their lives would change forever.

PART TWO
PREPARATION & SUPPLIES

PART TWO
PREPARATIONS AND SUPPLIES

Wednesday 9:00 a.m.

It was a brisk, bright morning when the little traffic light at the corner of Hansen and Heart woke up at the start of a new day. The traffic below where the little light lived had been very slow the evening before. This usually meant a few more hours of shut-eye for Rudy, Yonny and Gertie. Any time the little traffic light could hit the snooze button more than once, there was a golden opportunity to kick back. Rudy slept like a baby the night before, but Yonny and Gertie were already getting restless. The Human Race was only a few days away, and race strategy was becoming their main focus. Usually the three friends enjoyed a nice breakfast together, but not this morning. There would be no friendly chitchat or playtime for them today, for you see this was "supply day" for the big race.

Each year before The Human Race started, racing supplies had to be acquired by each contestant. Participants of the race took this preparation very seriously because it could mean the difference between winning and losing. Gertie still believed her idea to combine their leadership styles would work, but convincing her two friends would be a real test of her optimism. Preparation and gathering supplies was all part of the pre-race excitement, along with some playful teasing and sarcastic remarks.

"Good morning, losers," laughed Rudy.

"Good morning, stubborn boy," exclaimed Gertie. "Have you thought anymore about what I said yesterday?"

Rudy grinned and said, "Yes, I have, and I still think your idea stinks! Combine our leadership styles, yeah, right!"

"What about you, Yonny, what do you think?" Gertie was hoping Yonny would stand up for once, and declare that he thought it was a great idea.

"I really haven't given it any thought," replied Yonny.

"Figures," said Rudy. "Do you ever think for yourself?"

"Sure I do. I mean, I think I do. Er, I mean I hope I do. I mean yeah… maybe." Rudy laughed at Yonny's indecision, and started to make his exit down to the street below, where he would begin gathering his supplies. Yonny and Gertie watched him as he merrily skipped along toward town.

However, just before he was out of earshot, Rudy heard Gertie say, "I'll be happy to help you with your supply list, Rudy." This unusual offer stopped Rudy dead in his tracks. He immediately began to think it was some sort of trick.

"Why would you want to help me?" Rudy asked.

"Because I consider you one of my closest friends, and I know you can use the help," said Gertie.

Rudy was taken aback by this strange display of friendship, but he managed to remain calm and polite. "Thanks, but no thanks. I'll be fine on my own." Then he jumped into high gear and away he went. The three agreed to meet back at the signal box at 12:00 p.m. sharp. The lunchtime traffic was always busy and all three lights were equally important to make the little traffic light function properly.

After Rudy was gone, Gertie quickly began to put her game plan for gathering supplies into action. She had proactively created her agenda and to-do list weeks in advance. She was not going to be caught unprepared this year. While lacing up her running shoes for her morning errands, she noticed that Yonny wasn't making any attempt at all to begin his preparations. Gertie was surprised by this, and it began to bother her a little; didn't Yonny know time was short?

"Why aren't you getting ready to leave?" she asked.

"Oh, I figured I would get supplies a little later when things weren't so hectic," Yonny slowly said.

"Later?" exclaimed Gertie. "Later might be too late. Pay now or pay on race day!"

"Well, what do you think I should do?" asked Yonny.

"I know exactly what you should do, but I'm not you, Yonny." Gertie slowly began to explain assertiveness, and boldly declared, "On our journeys through life we have two choices. Choice one: Become a passenger. Choice two: Be the driver. If I tell you what I think you should do, you'll be nothing but a passenger, and who knows where that road may take you. You should take the driver's seat of life more often, Yonny; you'll get further that way."

Yonny looked closely at Gertie for a few moments, and then quietly said, "When we do not take responsibility for our own actions, we are riding shotgun through life. When we ride shot-gun, we have no control."

Gertie jumped up and said, "Exactly! Now you're thinking!"

Yonny began to feel more positive about his current situation. Supplies needed to be gathered and he was going to be the one to do it. After a few minutes of collecting his thoughts, he left Gertie and headed out on his personal quest for supplies. All the while, he kept repeating the same line over and over in his mind, "Be the driver, take control. Be the driver, take control. Be the driver, take control."

Meanwhile, Rudy was well on his way checking off

items from his supply list. He entered the hardware store shortly after 10 a.m. and headed straight for the flashlight aisle. After about 15 minutes of diligent searching, he finally found the perfect flashlight. In Rudy's mind, a flashlight and multiple packs of batteries were essential to winning The Human Race. He always heard, you can never have enough batteries. But for some reason he never did. This year, however, things were going to change. He decided that being prepared for the race was more important than anything else, and his take-charge attitude was beginning to surprise even him.

Upon leaving the hardware store he ran into some trouble, however. His old archenemy, One Way, was walking into the store just as he was walking out. The two eyed each other for a moment and then quickly looked away. Finally, One Way said, "Hello, Rudy. How's my autocratic, domineering, over-bearing, know-it-all, one-track-mind friend doing today?" Rudy said nothing, but quickly turned a bright shade of red that was very different from his normal coloring. He hated being called a know-it-all, and that was partly because he knew it was true. Rudy was in a hurry and did not have time to argue or answer back right now. He tried to let the comment slide, but One Way's taunt seemed to get the better of him.

"I'm fine," he responded. Then he fired back: "How are you, you pig-headed, one- way thinking, egotistical, boastful, arrogant piece of tin?" (As if either one had much room to talk!)

One Way could see Rudy's blood beginning to boil, so he decided to push his buttons even further. "What a nice thing to say!" answered One Way. "By the way, why are you shopping alone on this beautiful morning, I thought you couldn't go anywhere without Tweedledee and Tweedledum? How are those knuckleheads Gertie and Yonny, anyway?"

What happened next is still a mystery to Rudy, but for some strange reason he felt a tingling sensation in his chest that made him want to stick up for his two friends. Ordinarily he would have laughed along with One Way, and even made an additional smart aleck comment or two; but not today. Rudy realized that he was feeling different about things, and that scared him.

Rudy thought for a moment before finding the right words to say. When he was finally ready to address One Way he did so with poise and confidence. "I do not appreciate you calling my friends names. You can call me anything you want, but please leave them out of this."

One Way had never during their entire friendship (if that's what you want to call it) heard Rudy stand up for his friends the way he was now. "You're joking right?"

asked One Way. "You cannot be serious."

Rudy glared at One Way and said very assertively, "This is no joke. If I hear you mention Gertie or Yonny again, I'm going to turn you into a piece of scrap metal."

"Ok, ok, calm down Rudy, I meant no offense, I'm outta here," said One Way.

But as Rudy began to walk away he could have sworn he heard his old so-called-friend mumble under his breath, "You're getting soooooooooft Rudy."

Was Rudy getting soft? Personally he did not feel that way, but emotionally something was definitely happening to him. For the first time in a long while, he began to feel a warm and fuzzy connection with Gertie and Yonny. This feeling frightened him and he quickly dismissed it as nothing more than an upset stomach from last evening's dinner. Subconsciously, however, he was wondering if Gertie's comments the night before and her suggestions this morning were seeping into his mind. It was still too early to tell.

Wednesday 11:30 a.m.

Once he made up his mind to pursue a plan of action, things began looking up for Yonny. He had already visited the local grocery store for energy snacks, and now he was on his way to a nearby department store to pick up some new running shoes. Running shoes were a must during The Human Race. As far as supplies went, everyone said that if only one thing could be bought, running shoes should be it. Participants of the race knew that the terrain was treacherous and good running shoes were very important. Even Rudy admitted that running shoes were vital to winning, although he always went for flashlights and batteries first. Yonny was starting to feel more confident about today's adventure, and started checking the items off his supply list one by one.

As he continued to stroll merrily down Main Street (being careful not to be spotted by the humans) he noticed something shiny up ahead in the distance. He squinted his eyes to see better and soon realized that the thing he saw advancing toward him was shaped like an upside down triangle. Yonny thought to himself, It couldn't be who I think it is, could it? But as the upside down triangle got closer and closer, Yonny was able to make out the colors red and white, which could only mean one thing... his archrival, Ms. Yield Sign, was heading straight for him.

By this time, Gertie was halfway finished purchasing the items on her supply list. She had already been to the grocery store, hardware store, and bakery. Next stop was the pharmacy. Vitamins were an important supply for Gertie; she felt they helped her maintain stamina during The Human Race. Every year, it was part of her supply day ritual to stop by the pharmacy and stock up on vitamins. As she entered the store, she noticed a rectangular sign walking down one of the aisles next to her. She did a double take and was surprised to find that the rectangular piece of tin in the next aisle was none other than her good friend Sammy the speed limit sign.

"Long time no see," shouted Gertie.

Upon hearing her comment Sammy looked up with a big grin and said, "Well, I'll be a son of a speed limit sign, if it isn't Ms. Gertie the green light."

"In the metal," she giggled.

"How in the heck are you Gertie? It has been a long time since we've seen each other. Ever since they moved me way up the street from Hansen and Heart, it's been harder and harder to get together," said Sammy.

"Tell me about it! I've tried several times to get

down your way, but lately traffic has been crazy," she continued.

"You aren't kidding," responded Sammy. "Why just last week I caused five humans to get a speeding ticket. I guess it serves them right though, doing 52 mph in my 35 mph speed zone. Won't they ever learn?"

"Probably not," said Gertie. With that said, the two were soon hugging each other and reminiscing about old times. Sammy was interested to hear about Rudy and Yonnny. At the same time, Gertie made sure she inquired about Sammy's wife, who was 5 years his senior. Her name, by the way, was Susan the speed limit sign. (Can you guess what her speed limit is?)

Sammy was quite impressed with how much Gertie had gotten accomplished so far today. He praised her on her proactive planning and assertive style. He said she would make a great leader one day in the "real world," if she could only get there. But little did her friend know that even as they were speaking to one another, Gertie was already planning her strategy for victory. She did want to reach the real world some day, and she knew the only way that was going to happen was if she won The Human Race. And the only way that was going to happen was to get some help from two other would-be leaders she knew, by the names of Yonny and Rudy.

Back on Main Street, Yonny was quickly trying to make his way through the crowds. It was always a challenge not to be spotted by the humans and Yonny was very careful when it came to this. It was busy for 11:30 a.m., so for a minute he thought he might have been seeing things when he spotted the inverted triangle walking in his direction. To his dismay, he was not seeing things. Sure enough, up in the distance Ms. Yield sign was heading straight towards him. The two met face to face and said nothing for a moment or two.

Finally, Ms. Yield broke the ice and said, "Hi, Yo-Yo."

This was her nickname for Yonny and he hated it. Ever since they were kids, Ms. Yield called him that because she said he could never make a decision and was always wishy-washy. She said he was like a Yo-Yo, always going up and down, up and down, up and down. He knew there was some truth to this, but he still did not appreciate the nickname. Ms. Yield liked to pick on him, and it looked like today would be no exception.

"How's my little Yo-Yo of a friend doing on this fine day?" Yonny was starting to turn orange, because his bright yellow face was becoming red with anger. He was tired of her negative attitude and her constant teasing. He had to put a stop to it, but how could he do it? He dug down deep inside and found some courage to stand up for himself.

"You know, Ms. Yield, you and I are somewhat alike. You're pretty hesitant yourself sometimes. I mean look at yourself; you're a Yield sign for goodness sake! You don't know whether to stop or go." It was true; they were both caution signs for the humans.

Ms. Yield looked confused. She had never heard Yonny speak to her this way before, and it was like she was talking to a different light. "I may be cautious, but at least I am my own boss. You have to depend on Rudy and Gertie to function properly. Without them you're just a plain old single yellow light."

Her comment was valid, but it also made Yonny think. He did depend on Rudy and Gertie to do his job properly. Without all three lights, the little traffic light could not be effective. This actually made him feel important. He began to realize just how special his two friends were to him. It took all three of their leadership attributes to be a team.

"You're right about that, Ms. Yield. I do depend on my friends and I'm thankful for it! Haven't you ever depended on someone before?" Yonny was feeling fantastic inside and he thought he knew why. He was finally beginning to understand the importance of INTERDEPENDENCY.

"What do you say we put all this negativity behind us?" Yonny boldly stated.

"What did you say?" asked Ms. Yield. She couldn't believe her ears.

"You heard me, why don't we become civil with each other. After all, we do have the same job."

Ms. Yield looked at him for a moment and then shyly said, "OK, I mean I think, I mean it might be a good idea. What do you think"?

"I already told you what I thought," Yonny said confidently. "Start thinking for yourself, Ms. Yield, you'll get further that way."

Now Yonny could not believe his own ears. Was he really saying what he thought he was saying? Maybe Gertie's optimistic comments were finally sinking in. He sure hoped so. Yonny looked at Ms. Yield and told her, "Be The Driver!" She smiled and said she would sure try. Yonny gently said goodbye to his friend, and realized he was beginning to feel something he had not felt for a long, long time... confidence!

Wednesday 5:00 p.m.

After leaving the pharmacy, Gertie noticed what appeared to be a curious human staring at her. It was impossible, she thought, there is no way a human could see her, she was too cautious to be seen. Anyhow, how would a human even know what they were looking at if they did spot her? All they would see is an old green light that appeared to be broken and no longer functioning. Still, it really did look like the man was watching her curiously. She picked up her pace, thought nothing of it and continued her journey back to the intersection of Hansen and Heart.

Meanwhile, Rudy was already back at the intersection loading his supplies into the new backpack he'd picked up at the sporting goods store. He still needed a few more things, like extra batteries, but they could wait until tomorrow. Tonight would be a busy night. Wednesday nights were always busy at the intersection of Hansen and Heart. Wednesdays were "dinner" night for the humans. It seemed that most humans would eat out on Wednesdays and therefore traffic would be stop and go the entire evening. Oh well, thought Rudy, only a few more days until the little traffic light goes "out of order" for the weekend. Every year around this time the little traffic light would mysteriously go out of service for a few days. The unsuspecting humans never picked up on this annual phenomenon, but Rudy, Yonny and Gertie could not participate in The Human Race unless it did.

Rudy looked down at his watch and realized that his two friends might be late getting back. He began thinking to himself, this is why I have to do things my way. If I depend on those two bozos I'll never win The Human Race. Just as he finished that thought, Gertie showed up.

"Hello Rudy," exclaimed Gertie. "How was your supply day?"

"My day was fine, but it seems that Yonny the slow poke is going to be late. When will that boy ever learn to tell time? He's the biggest procrastinator I know."

"He may be a little slow, but his intentions are good," said Gertie.

"Intentions won't make the traffic light turn yellow,"

shouted Rudy. "Without Yonny we're going to have to become out of order early, and that may cause suspicion from the humans."

Gertie realized this to be true and she began to worry slightly about Yonny. Just as Rudy was about to complain some more, Yonny showed up.

"Hi ya guys!" Yonny merrily said.

"Don't hi me, late bloomer, you're late!" said Rudy.

"I know. I'm sorry, but I can explain." said Yonny.

"This should be good!" laughed Rudy.

Yonny began explaining how he ran into Ms. Yield sign and how the two of them decided to work out their differences and become friends.

"How did that happen?" inquired Gertie curiously.

Rudy rudely interrupted, "I'm sure it's a very touching story, but we have work to do, so you'll have to share your story later."

With that said, the three jumped back into the signal box and started functioning together as a working traffic light. Cars came and went and the little traffic light was busy the rest of the evening.

After about two hours of non-stop blinking and flashing, Yonny looked down at Gertie and simply said, "I became the driver today and it felt great!" Gertie whispered up, "I'm proud of you Yonny, I knew you had it in you." Yonny blushed with delight.

Wednesday 8:00 p.m.

The traffic that night at the corner of Hansen and Heart was busy, busy, busy.

Rudy, Yonny and Gertie continued to flash red, yellow and green non-stop. At around 9 p.m. traffic would slow down for about two or three hours, before the humans made their mad dashes home for the evening. It was only 8 p.m. and the three were already getting tired. They worked without conversation for the next hour until no more headlights could be seen coming in any direction. Finally, it was time to relax.

Gertie broke the silence and said, "I'm going to go out for a bite to eat, would you two like to join me?" Yonny responded that he wasn't hungry and Rudy said he would rather eat alone. With that said, Gertie made her way down to the street and started heading north. She was in the mood for a burger and fries, but knew she was going to probably have to settle for a coffee and doughnut. The nearest burger joint was almost five miles away, and Gertie knew she would not have enough time to get there and back before she had to return to the traffic signal. She laced up her running shoes and started moving out. But as she began trotting down the street she felt as if someone was following her.

"That's silly," she thought, "Why would someone

follow me?" She told herself to stop being paranoid and continued on with her journey. After about 15 minutes, however, she realized that she wasn't being paranoid; someone was following her and it wasn't another traffic light or sign…it was a human!

By this time, Rudy and Yonny had gone their separate ways and were each heading out for a bite to eat. Rudy decided he wanted to eat alone tonight and Yonny made no effort to join him. With only one more day of preparation left, everyone had their mind on their own agendas. Rudy settled for a slice of pizza, and Yonny found himself in front of a local taco stand. Tomorrow's dinner would definitely have to be more nutritious. Being in tip-top shape, both physically and mentally, was crucial for winning The Human Race. Rudy gobbled down his pizza in only a few minutes. He was a fast eater. In fact, it always seemed like he had to do things in a hurry. This attribute made him very different from his two friends. He was an aggressive kind of person who thought making quick decisions without asking for help from others was the way to live life. His stubborn ideas on aggressive leadership and being the boss were the reason he had been labeled a domineering personality, but this suited him just fine. He quickly walked back home and began testing his new flashlight.

After Yonny finished eating his tacos, he was ready to head back to the corner when all of a sudden he realized he had forgotten something very important… running shoes! How could he let this happen? Without proper running shoes he could never compete. Oh well he thought, there is always tomorrow. But then again, it seemed as if he was always putting things off until tomorrow. His behavior pattern was one of *I'll get to that later*. He disregarded all his worries for another day and headed for home. As he was walking along, however, he thought of the phrase Be the Driver and how he decided not to apply it on this evening. There was always tomorrow.

Just a few blocks away Gertie was still in pursuit of her donut and coffee. A human following me? This cannot be happening, thought Gertie. But it was. The human appeared to be the same human that she saw earlier in the day. Gertie quickly made a right turn on the next street and then a quick left on the following street. Then she doubled back and retraced the same route two more times. After about a half-hour of walking, the human was nowhere in sight. Gertie stepped up the pace and headed home. Tomorrow was going to be a big day.

Sending Signals

The little traffic light woke up to a warm and sunny Thursday morning. It was already 65 degrees outside and it was only going to get hotter. Today was the last day for preparation and gathering supplies for The Human Race that started on Friday. Rudy, Yonny and Gertie each realized that in a few days they could actually be human, and this thought both excited and scared them. Could they even survive as humans? What would their lives be like in that very strange and very different world? Only time would tell.

"Good morning," yawned Gertie. She was usually the first one to wake up. She was surprised when she noticed Rudy was already up and gone.

"Where's Rudy?" she asked.

"Where do you think? He went out to get more batteries!" exclaimed Yonny.

"How many batteries does one little light need?" laughed Gertie.

"You know him, he's a fanatic about this stuff," said Yonny. Fanatic or not, Gertie just hoped Rudy would make it back on time before the morning traffic became heavy. She realized that they needed him on the job when things got busy.

After eating a quick breakfast, Yonny and Gertie got up into the metal casing of the traffic light and assumed their working position. The morning traffic started around 9 a.m. and ended at 10 a.m. At about 8:55 a.m. Rudy showed up with two shopping bags and a new backpack.

"Nice of you to join us," said Gertie sarcastically.

"Yeah, yeah, yeah," said Rudy dismissively.

"Better late than never," said the newly upbeat Yonny. The three lights worked non-stop for the next hour as cars came by one after the other.

Sending Signals

Thursday 10:15 a.m.

The morning rush hour traffic was over and it was time for a break. The final day for preparation was here and each of our three friends had a few more items to pick up before they could put their supply lists away. Yonny needed some snacks and running shoes, Rudy needed to stop by the pharmacy, and Gertie needed a new sweatshirt. With only one day left before The Human Race, everything had to be in apple-pie order.

Gertie slowly made her way over to her friends and asked hesitantly, "So…are we going to combine our leadership skills and win this thing?"

"I'm not sure," said Yonny, "I really haven't given it much thought."

Rudy responded in his typical sarcastic manner, "No way, not going to happen!"

"Just think about it, okay?," said Gertie, and off she

went to the clothing store.

"I'm hungry," moaned Yonny. "I think I'm in the mood for tacos today"

"You're always in the mood for tacos," said Rudy.

"Oh, like you have room to talk, pizza boy."

"Hey, you leave my pizza out of this," said Rudy. "Pizza is a nutritional part of any balanced diet."

"Yeah, if you're in college and have no money," laughed Yonny.

Soon the two were on their way to gather up the final supplies needed. Yonny headed over to the shoe store, while Rudy made his way to the pharmacy.

The clothing store was packed with humans everywhere. It was a busy day and this presented a problem for Gertie; she couldn't even see the "secret passage" that led down to the basement. If she couldn't get to the basement today, she would be in big trouble.

It is a little known fact that all the lights and signs

that compete in The Human Race have secret places to buy their goods. (How else did you think they did it? You didn't actually think they walked up to a register and placed their merchandise on the counter, did you?) These secret spots are run by the Detour Signs. The Detour Signs have been in business for years, and are the sole suppliers of the race. Whenever they need supplies, they mysteriously appear out of nowhere and cause a "detour." Then the human driving the supply truck takes the detour and eventually gets lost. Whenever the driver stops to ask for directions, the Detour Signs "borrow" the items they need.

Detouring is a system that has kept them in business from the start. Of course, they are honest enough to pay for what they take. (I knew you were wondering about that). Haven't you ever wondered where all the coins you drop go? Well, now you know. The Detour Signs collect them and leave them on the driver's seat.

When the driver returns to the truck, the merchandise is gone, but there just enough money to cover the driver's losses. Next time you see a detour sign, reach for your map and watch your wallet!

After 30 minutes of waiting around, an opening to the secret passage finally appeared. Gertie jumped at the opportunity and scrambled for the basement. Once she reached the last step, she relaxed a little and made her way over to the sweatshirt department. Just as she figured: all of the black ones were gone! She settled for a brown and blue striped sweatshirt and walked to the register.

"Hi ya Gertie!" said Danny the Detour Sign. "Long time no see. Did you find everything you needed?"

"Yes I did, thanks for asking," replied Gertie.

"Your friend Rudy was in here earlier" said Danny. "He bought the last black sweatshirt we had. Maybe he'll share it with you?"

"Fat chance that will happen! Just this one for me," exclaimed Gertie. She paid for her sweatshirt and then left, calling back a "See ya later" to Danny.

The morning sun beat down on Gertie as she cautiously left the store. She was about a half a block away when she felt something wasn't right. Out of the corner of her eye she spotted a human staring at her. Not again she thought. She quickened her pace and glanced over her shoulder. She couldn't believe her eyes, it was the same human she had seen the other day! This is strange, she mumbled to herself, and then made a mad dash for the alley behind the store. The human did not follow her this time, but instead stood on the corner and began reading a book. Gertie waited for nearly an hour before the coast was clear. When she finally left the alley it was time to return home.

Thursday 11:45 a.m.

The line at the grocery store looked endless. Yonny was patiently waiting his turn when he noticed the time. He had to be back at the corner of Hansen and Heart by noon, and he still hadn't visited the shoe store. If only he would have gotten there yesterday, he lamented to himself. His procrastination was causing him anxiety. How was he ever going to win The Human Race if he couldn't even get the supplies he needed? Oh well, there was always next year.

Nearby, Rudy continued to gather supplies. "I'll take one bottle of aspirin and two rolls of Vitamin C tablets," said Rudy. The Detour pharmacist handed a bag to Rudy and he was on his way. A few more packs of batteries and he was finished. While he was walking down the street he ran into One Way.

"Hey, One Way, how's life treating you?"

"It's good, but it'll be even better once I win the race."

Rudy looked at him and said, "You have to beat me first."

"No problem," said One Way. "You'll be so worried about Gertie and Yonny during the race that you won't have time to win."

Rudy looked confused. "What are you talking about? Why would I worry about those two ding-dongs?"

One Way laughed, "I'm glad to see you have your sense of humor back."

"It never left," said Rudy. "I just had an upset stomach when I last saw you. Tell me what you're talking about."

"The word on the street is that You, Yonny and Gertie are going to combine your leadership talents to win The Human Race."

"Are you crazy?" yelled Rudy, "I never said I would

do that."

One Way looked at him and said, "I'm just telling you what I've heard."

"Well you've heard wrong!" said Rudy.

One Way could see that Rudy was upset, and even though they were not good friends he said he would squelch the rumor.

"Thanks, One Way, I owe you one."

One Way smiled mischeviously and said, "I won't let you forget."

Sending Signals

The afternoon traffic was finished when Rudy made an effort to speak with Gertie.

"What on earth have you been telling people?" demanded Rudy.

"What are you talking about?" said Gertie.

Rudy looked at her and said, "I'm talking about how everyone thinks we're going to be a team for The Human Race."

Gertie smiled and responded, "We are? That's great news! I was hoping you would come around."

"Ha, ha, very funny," said Rudy. "I mean the lights and signs are saying it, not me!"

Gertie leaned into him and said, "Well, it's a good idea if I do say so myself. Are you sure you're not interested?"

Rudy threw up his hands and stormed out. The last

thing he heard Gertie say before he left was, "See ya later, teammate!"

Yonny looked down at his watch and decided that right now was the time to buy his running shoes. It was the final supply he needed. The Human Race started tomorrow at noon. Forty-eight hours was a long time to be on one's feet and proper running shoes were a must. He said his goodbye to Gertie and began the long seven-mile walk to the shoe store.

The secret passageway to the basement of the shoe store was clear when Yonny arrived. He jogged down the steps and headed for the aisle with his size. Under a pile of boxes, he found a pair of comfortable shoes and headed quickly to the checkout line. Ms. Yield sign was also shopping at this time, and the two were in line together. "Hi Yo-Y... I mean Yonny. How have you been?"

Yonny smiled, "I'm great, thanks for asking."

Ms. Yield sign looked away and then hesitantly asked, "Is it true what I've been hearing?"

"Depends on what you've been hearing," said Yonny.

"Are you, Rudy and Gertie really going to combine your leadership abilities during The Human Race?" asked Ms. Yield.

Yonny looked down, "I honestly don't know. The idea sounds okay, but I haven't really given it much thought."

Ms. Yield tapped him on the shoulder and said, "I knew you were still a Yo-Yo! If I had the chance to get help from my friends, I would take it in a heartbeat. You wouldn't catch me being wishy-washy." Ms. Yield walked away and mumbled under her breath loud enough for Yonny to hear, "Have a nice trip as the passenger." Yonny tried to catch up with her to ask what she meant by that, but by then she was gone. He was sure that everything would work out some way or another, but wondered why everyone was talking about them. He shrugged to himself, then left the shoe store and headed for home.

Rudy walked over three miles before he began to tire. All his supplies were accounted for and he was certain he had plenty of batteries. He still couldn't believe that Gertie was not giving up on the idea of combining their leadership skills. Her philosophy seemed silly to him. If he was going to win the race he had to be in total control.

He was almost back home when he suddenly decided to grab an early dinner. Pizza sounded great to him- it always did! Although the secret passage to the pizza shop was crowded, he managed to squeeze in and place his order for a double pepperoni with extra cheese. He enjoyed his pepperoni pizza in silence.

Meanwhile, Gertie had successfully gathered all the

supplies she needed. Her checklist was completed, but she still had nagging doubts. Her idea about "creating a team" was the key to victory, but she finally came to the conclusion that it might not happen. She wondered what she was doing wrong. Why couldn't she convince her friends to buy into her plan? Was she too aggressive? Was she too passive? There had to be an explanation, but darned if she knew what it was. She spent the rest of the afternoon resting and hoping for a miracle.

Thursday 8:00 p.m.

When the evening traffic finally slowed down, Gertie and Yonny set out to get a quick bite to eat. Rudy remained back at the corner and stubbornly ate his leftover pizza. The conversation between Yonny and Gertie was light, but they were both focusing on one thing. Both the taco stand and donut shop were frequented while they chatted. After their bellies were full they headed back home.

Tonight was the last night the little traffic light would be in working order for a few days. Each year at the stroke of midnight on the eve of The Human Race, the traffic light would mysteriously stop functioning. This year would be no different.

Rudy had just finished packing when Yonny and Gertie arrived back home. "How was dinner? Let me guess…a taco for the late bloomer and a donut for Ms. crazy idea. You two will never change."

Just as Rudy was finishing his sentence Gertie stood up and wiped a little pizza sauce off his face. "I guess you're right. None of us will change if we don't win this race." The three of them rested for the next few hours.

Sending Signals

When the last car drove out of sight Rudy, Yonny and Gertie jumped out of the metal casing they called home. Realistically this could be the last time they would ever sleep there again. In a few days they would know for sure. With only one more hour until bedtime, last minute checks were being made.

Gertie was checking her list for the third time while Rudy and Yonny were looking at theirs for the first time. Gertie's assertiveness allowed her to remain somewhat calmer than her two friends. While they were frantically checking off items, she just sat back and relaxed. She asked if they needed help but Yonny said no and Rudy just grunted. For the next hour they made their final preparations and then got ready for bed.

Friday 12:00 a.m.

The clock struck midnight, and as scheduled, the little traffic light went out of order. Rudy, Yonny and Gertie settled down for a peaceful night's sleep. Because the light would be out of order, they had the opportunity to sleep in until it was time to leave. All of the planning that went into winning the race was complete. Tomorrow they would get their maps and be on their way. There were no directions to memorize because each year they were different.

Gertie yawned, "Sleep tight, don't let the rust bugs bite, and think about what I said about combining our leadership styles."

Yonny sleepily said, "Good night."

Rudy decided not to respond, but instead, mumbled something underneath his breath. They all shut their eyes and slowly drifted off to sleep.

PART THREE
THE HUMAN RACE

PART THREE
THE HUMAN RACE

Friday 12:00 p.m.

The afternoon air had a faint autumn chill, as the energy around the starting area was slowly gaining momentum. The families of the participants found their spots along the starting line and waited in eager anticipation. Everyone was excited about what the future might hold for the winner, and anxious about the inevitable disappointment of the losers. The participants knew that if they won the race, they would not be returning to their normal life as a sign or signal. This knowledge both motivated and scared them.

The officials signaled the kickoff of the race with a loud BANG from the starter pistol, and the runners were off! The Human Race was finally on its way and jockeying for position began immediately. Yonny decided he was going to hang in the back of the pack and conserve his strength for the finish. He figured he had plenty of time to plan out a strategy once the leaders and followers were sorted out. Gertie decided to stay up with the front of the pack, so she could be prepared to make her move when the time was right. Rudy decided he wasn't even going to run with the pack, and he made the peculiar decision to go in another direction completely. He was thinking to himself, if I'm going to win, I have to do it my way!

For the first few hours most of the participants paced themselves carefully and waited for a sign that the leaders were making a push. No one wanted to get tired early in the race, and have nothing left at the finish. With almost 46 1/2 hours to go, conserving energy was important.

Part Three — The Human Race

Friday 2:00 p.m.

By now, each runner had their own idea of how they wanted to proceed during the race. Earlier that morning, they had received their roadmaps and studied them intensely. Now that the race was actually under way, all their plans and strategies had to be put into practice.

Our friend Gertie decided that she was going to take a ferry across one of the lakes that dotted the map. Participants had the choice of either going around the lakes or over them. She felt the productive thing would be to jump on a ferry and cross while she rested and saved herself for the finish.

Her proactive thinking paid off. She made her move, and very quickly was sitting aboard a ferry that had approached the dock just a few minutes before. She snuck into the storage facility on the bottom deck and waited out the 30 minute journey, thinking ahead. When the boat reached the opposite shore, she sprang off and headed for her next destination. Before she exited, however, she noticed something strange. It was a human watching her again. Not just any ordinary human, but the *same* one she had been seeing the past few days. She couldn't believe her eyes. Why was he watching her like that? She didn't stick around to find out. As soon as she stepped off the ferry, she kicked up her heels and dashed off; she was out of sight and so was he.

Meanwhile, our friend Yonny was proceeding very slowly. Instead of using the ferry like Gertie, he decided it would be best to walk around the lake. He figured he had plenty of time to waste. What was a few extra hours strolling around the lake going to hurt in the long run? While walking along the path around the lake, he ran into some of the other competitors, his friend Ms.

Yield among them.

"Hi Yonny," said Ms. Yield.

"How's it going?" asked Yonny.

"I'm getting tired already!" exclaimed Ms. Yield. "I need a rest stop." Yonny knew exactly how she felt, and decided to sit and talk with her for a while. Yonny never saw what was coming. Little did he suspect that Ms. Yield's tiredness and endless procrastination were going to bog him down for hours. Yonny's friend had to sit and rest, so he unquestioningly adopted her choice. Her "I'll get to it later" mentality fit him to a "t," so he went right along with it. They had planned to rest for just a little bit, but of course they took much longer. They napped for a while, and when they finally woke up, reality set in: they were hours behind! How could they have let this happen? Yonny estimated that he was at least one and a half hours behind Gertie up at the front. Ms. Yield and Yonny blamed each other, and decided to go their separate ways as the guilt ate at them both.

By this time, Rudy had already crossed the lake following his own route. He didn't take the ferry or walk around the lake, but instead, hid in the backseat of a nearby motorboat. The boat made it across the lake in no time at all, and he was off and running. He knew he was only a few minutes behind Gertie, but this did not bother him. In his mind, she was bound to make a mistake soon.

The traffic lights and road signs were spread out along the race course by now, and all of them positioned themselves in comparison to the one in front and in back. The participants were a good five hours into the race, but they still were saving their strength because they knew that if they didn't, they would come up short at the finish. It was starting to cool down considerably, and this meant that it would be getting dark soon.

Flashlights were being checked, batteries were tested, and maps were being pored over anxiously in the twilight.

After Rudy reached the other side of the lake he took a chance on a short cut, and his contrarian choice soon had him lost. He ended up going two miles out of his way, which made him angry, because he had been doing so well. Now Gertie and some of the others were way ahead of him. "Not to worry," he thought to himself; night was coming on and that was his favorite time of the race. When others were stumbling around and getting lost in the dark, Rudy, along with his trusty flashlight and extra supply of batteries, would make good time.

Rudy was finally heading in the right direction down a one-way street, and his spirits were picking up, when he ran into more misfortune. An unexpected booby-trap was lying in wait for him. Not knowing the area well, he stumbled and fell into what appeared to be a gigantic pothole, but off the path in the middle of the woods! Great, he thought, how in the heck am I going to get out of this one? Just as he finished that thought, a face appeared above him and looked down into the hole at him.

"Hi ya, Rudy," sneered One Way. "Are you falling for me?" he asked sarcastically.

"Very funny, now help me out of here!" yelled Rudy angrily.

"Sorry, I can't do that. You see, if I help you out now, then you might just win the race and we don't want that to happen now do we?" Rudy was furious and his face showed it. One Way said he was sorry he had to cheat, but it was all part of his plan. As he was leaving he quietly said to himself, "I sure hope Yonny, Gertie, and the rest of the bunch are as easy to trick as you were."

Rudy was now all by himself, without friends or directions or roadmaps, and for the first time in a long while, he was afraid.

Gertie, on the other hand, was making good time and was even further along than she had hoped. She decided to take a short rest as the sun began to set. She closed her eyes for a moment and began wondering about Yonny and Rudy. She hoped they were safe, and wished them the best.

Friday 7:00 p.m.

Yonny was finally back on schedule, or at least as close as he was comfortable with. His little nap had made him feel more energized, and he was ready to travel all through the night. He was about to stop for a quick bite to eat when he heard a rustling sound coming from the bushes up ahead in the distance. Must be a squirrel, he thought, and kept moving towards the sound. Before he even realized what was happening, a large net was being hurled over his head. He hit the ground and started to panic, trying to wiggle out of it, but it was no use. While he lay on the ground oblivious to what had just happened, he looked up and saw the faint resemblance of an arrow pointing in one direction. One Way had just captured his next victim.

Gertie was making real progress, and was currently one of the leaders of the race. She realized that her preparation and planning was paying off. She figured out her strategy early on, and her optimistic attitude was having the usual effect. She was starting to actually believe she might have a chance of winning this thing. She was getting hungry, though, and decided to take a quick break in a nearby park to eat one of her delicious blueberry donuts. They always made her feel happy. She found a nice secluded park bench and sat down and began munching on her donut.

As she plopped the last bite into her mouth, Gertie decided it was time to move on. Just as she was about to leave the park, a human stepped into the path ahead. She froze, and quickly settled back down onto the park bench. She began breathing deeply as the sweat beads rolled off her forehead. It can't be, she thought, it just can't be. But it was. The human who was now in her sights had been the same one she had been seeing for the past few days. It's over, she thought. That man is on to me and he will discover that I'm not a real traffic light. When that happens, I'll be scrap metal. Just as she was about to give up and run away into the woods, the human sat down next to her. He said nothing. This silence made Gertie even more nervous, but she figure that if she didn't attract attention he might ignore her and go away.

Meanwhile Rudy was still stuck in the trap that had

been set by his old buddy One Way. Rudy wished he had some help, but he knew that was not going to arrive anytime soon. Most of the competitors were well past his location and the spectators weren't lined up on this part of the track. At least he still had his black sweatshirt disguise, he thought, then quickly realized it would do him no good in a black hole. Thank goodness he had plenty of batteries to help get him through the night. He decided to get some rest and figure a way out of the hole in the morning. He could still win this race if he got out early, but he was going to need some help. As he laid his head down to rest, he could hear the words coming from Gertie's mouth loud and clear. How about we help each other and win this race together. He shut his eyes, thought about his smarty-pants answer the other day, and knew he had made a mistake.

Yonny, trapped in One Way's net and unable to move, was about ready to give up completely when he heard some familiar voices coming his way. It was Danny the Detour Sign and a few of his buddies! Yonny felt relief and started to call out to them. Within a couple of minutes Danny and his friends found Yonny and helped to untangle him from the net. When Yonny was finally free, he gave each sign a great big hug and thanked them over and over.

"No problem," said Danny. "We are all about helping each other."

"I didn't know you ever competed in The Human Race," said Yonny.

"I usually don't, but I figured if I could run a successful business underground, imagine what I could do above ground! If I win, I win; if I lose, I lose. Either way I'm still going to be in business," explained Danny.

"You'll always have me as a customer!" exclaimed Yonny. Danny smiled and said goodbye, then continued down along the path that he and his friends were certain (or at least hoped) would lead them to victory.

Meanwhile, the human on the park bench next to Gertie just sat there staring straight ahead and smiling. Gertie decided it would be best to go into "shut down mode." If the human thought she were just an old broken down traffic light, maybe he would leave her alone. Then she realized that old broken down traffic lights don't just plop themselves down on a park bench everyday. Nonetheless, she had no choice but to stay where she was, keep quiet and hope for the best.

Then suddenly the human looked over at her and nodded his head. He knows I'm alive, thought Gertie, but how? The smiling stopped and the human began to look more seriously at Gertie. This is it, she thought, I'm a goner now. Gertie was beginning to think her optimistic attitude wouldn't get her out of this one, when all of a sudden, the human stood up and left! She couldn't believe it; he just got up and walked away!

She sat there, frozen still, while the human continued to walk away. Then she noticed that he stopped just before he was out of sight and looked back at her. He smiled and called out, "Good luck, by the way, my name's Randy." Gertie could not believe her ears. For the first time in her entire life she actually had a human speak directly to her. When the human was far enough away she jumped to her feet and headed for the park exit. As she was getting ready to leave she glanced over her shoulder at the park bench that she and the human were just sitting on moments ago. She saw something that made her stop dead in her tracks. She couldn't believe her eyes! On the bench where they had been sitting was now lay a small brown leather journal. She moved closer to examine the object and noticed the date 1954 inscribed on the cover. 1954, she thought. What in the heck would a human like that be doing with a journal from…..and then it hit her; this was the legendary secret journal! A chill sent its way down the back of her spine as she came to the realization that the human who had been watching had, once upon a time, been just like her and her friends.

Friday 10:00 p.m.

Night had fallen, his flashlight was still on, and Rudy was wide-awake. Batteries would be all-important tonight. He knew he should probably get some rest, but he couldn't stop thinking about how he was going to get out of his current situation. By this time the other competitors were way ahead of him, and his chances of winning were fading fast. His leadership philosophy of being the "one in charge" and "my way or the highway" wasn't helping him much now, because he was off the beaten path and lost in a dark hole in a strange place.

Meanwhile, Yonny was happy to be out of the trap set by One Way. He still couldn't understand why One Way would pick on him and not Rudy...unless...he already had caught Rudy! Could Rudy be in trouble somewhere, and no one knew about it? Yonny decided he was going to find out. He knew back tracking would cost him precious time, but for some unexplainable reason he felt compelled to help his friend. Yonny started jogging back in the direction where he had seen One Way emerge from the bushes. If One Way had done something to Rudy, Yonny would find him nearby. With his new running shoes laced up tight, Yonny was making great time and could spare a moment to help a friend. After about 40 minutes of crossing treacherous terrain, he stumbled upon what appeared to be a clearing. Why would there be a clearing in the middle of the woods, he wondered. Within minutes he found the answer. About 15 feet away, he could see the faint beam of a flashlight coming from a large hole. When he peered down inside, he got quite a surprise. Rudy was sitting in the middle of the hole opening another pack of batteries. Rudy slowly looked up at his friend, smiled and said, "What took you so long?" They both laughed.

Not too far away Gertie was still in shock. Was she really in possession of the secret journal that was used to win The Human Race back in 1954? It looked so small and thin. How could there be a strategy written within the pages of this journal when it seemed so lightweight? When she opened the journal to the first page, she quickly found out. In big bold letters in the middle of the page were the words: **Become Colorblind**. Gertie was confused at first. Become colorblind? Was that the strategy? How could that one phrase, one idea, help an old traffic light win the race?

As she continued to flip through the pages of the

journal she found they were all blank. She couldn't believe there was nothing else written. No preparation planning, no map navigation, no supply list, nothing. Then it hit her, Become Colorblind must mean that we should accept everyone for their own uniqueness. It was true, she reflected, that she, Gertie, was a "green" light and always pro-active; Yonny was a "yellow" light and very passive; Rudy was a "red" light and always aggressive. But when you took away their different glass color lenses, they were all just lights. As individuals, we should stop searching for the differences in other's leadership styles and start focusing on the strengths and similarities of the group members.

At that moment, Gertie realized that maybe even she was a bit guilty when it came to finding fault with her two friends. She had always thought of Rudy as moody and autocratic, and that was what she resented the most. When she thought of Yonny she perceived him as tentative and somewhat lazy. Now, with this illuminating new information, she could see that both of her friends offered strong leadership qualities as well. Rudy took charge, and sometimes that was a good thing. Yonny liked to think things through, mulling things over, and that could be good too. She came back to the same conclusion she had almost given up on: all three leadership styles were important and necessary for winning The Human Race. She couldn't wait to find her two friends and share the good news with them!

Saturday 12:00 a.m.

Yonny had Rudy out of the hole in no time at all. To Yonny's surprise, Rudy actually thanked him for his efforts.

"We make a pretty good team," said Yonny.

Rudy gave his typical reply, "Don't get too comfortable buddy. I may like being your friend, but your teammate I'm not."

Yonny said nothing, but instead just winked at him.

"What are you winking at?" demanded Rudy.

"Just the best darn teammate in the whole wide world!" exclaimed Yonny.

Rudy reddened a little, and said simply, "You exhaust my patience…"

"What are teammates for," responded Yonny. For the next few minutes they sat there thinking about what needed to be done next. Then, almost simultaneously they both said, "I wonder how Gertie is doing?"

Yonny and Rudy decided that it would be best to rest for the night and get a fresh start in the morning, when things were clearer. Before they drifted off to sleep, Rudy checked his flashlight and batteries one more time. Little did Yonny know, but as soon as he fell asleep, Rudy would be heading out on his own again. He realized his friend Yonny would be upset, and that was too bad, but Rudy still felt he needed to win the race his way. If Yonny were tagging along, it would only slow him down. Yonny, on the other hand, had his own game plan, and when an exhausted Rudy woke up the next day he was in for a little surprise himself.

Yonny figured that Rudy might try to sneak away, so before he went to bed he set up a little alarm system to warn him when Rudy was leaving. Yonny had secretly tied a piece of string around Rudy's backpack. When Rudy pulled the pack, the string would tug on Yonny's shoelace indicating that Rudy was taking off. The plan worked perfectly. After about an hour of pretending to be asleep, Rudy got up and moved out silently, but Yonny was up and following right behind him.

Gertie was on a mission now, and that mission was to find her two friends and explain the secret journal left by a human named Randy. There was no doubt in her mind that the human Randy was once probably just like her friend Rudy the red light. Gertie only hoped that she could convince Rudy to change before it was too late. Gertie looked up at the night sky; the full moon was shining bright, so she said a little prayer that she would find her friends safe and sound. Gertie knew that tomorrow was going to be a long day, so she lay down to catch a few hours of shut-eye before morning.

Saturday 8:00 a.m.

Rudy made excellent time all through the night, staring straight ahead into the dark. By dawn, he was well on his way to catching up with the other competitors. He wished he could find One Way and teach him a lesson, but he realized that winning the race and becoming human would be the sweetest revenge of all. Rudy was steadily gaining momentum, but no more than 50 yards behind him was our good friend Yonny, tagging along. Yonny was starting to second-guess his decision to follow Rudy. He was getting extremely tired again, but knew he could not rest until Rudy finally decided to stop. Yonny hoped that would be very soon.

Meanwhile, Danny the Detour Sign and his buddies had already given up hope of winning. They were so lost it wasn't funny. Instead of packing it up and quitting, however, Danny decided he was going to conduct some business on the side. After all, he was the main supplier of goods and services to the traffic lights and road signs. Why go home when you could make a few bucks selling merchandise at the race? This was a whole new concept for him and his employees. Every year they would supply the competitors of The Human Race before hand, but this year they would supply racers during the race and double their race week profits. If they could only find the race course again!

Once Danny and his partners found their way back to what appeared to be race course territory, they set up shop and started selling like mad. Competitors stopped in their tracks to restock their supplies, then went right back on track. They were happy, and so were Danny and his boys.

Danny was grinning and counting his money when he noticed One Way looking strangely at some merchandise.

"What are you doing here?" asked Danny.

One Way sneered: "Just looking at this garbage for sale."

Danny lashed back, "Bite your tongue, tin boy. You don't have to shop here if you don't want to."

One Way knew that he shouldn't push Danny's hot buttons. In fact everyone knew that when Danny got upset, you had better watch out.

"I'm looking for a black sweatshirt," said One Way.

"Sorry Charley, all sold out. Your buddy Rudy bought the last one."

"Oh, is that right? Well, he won't be needing it where he is now," laughed One Way. Danny didn't even have to ask; he knew One Way was up to something and it wasn't good.

By this time Gertie was well on her way to rejoining the front of the pack. She had made great time the day before, and to top it off had a wonderful night's sleep. She was fresh and rearing to go! She still wondered about Yonny and Rudy, but was positive that she would find them before it was too late. She wanted badly to win the race, but she wanted to do it with her two friends at her side.

Gertie moved briskly ahead in the certainty that

she would eventually run into Yonny and Rudy. While crossing a large bridge Gertie spotted Sammy the speed limit sign up ahead in the distance. She ran full speed to catch up with him, and was quite exhausted when she finally reached him.

"Hi ya Sammy," said Gertie cheerily.

"How's my favorite green light doing on this fine morning?" responded Sammy.

"I'm ok, but I would be a lot better if I knew where Rudy and Yonny were."

Sammy stared cautiously at Gertie for a moment and then said, "I don't want to cause you worry, but I was just visiting with Danny and his buddies, who by the way have set up a merchandise stand in the middle of the forest. They said One Way was there and acting suspicious. It could be nothing, but I'm not sure."

Gertie froze where she was and with a look of concern on her face asked, "What do you mean by suspicious?"

"Well, One Way wanted to buy a black sweatshirt and Danny told him that Rudy bought the last one. After One Way heard this, he laughed and told Danny that Rudy wouldn't be needing it where he was."

"I can't believe it," said Gertie. "Why would One Way say that? What did he mean?" In her gut, however, she knew the answer to her own question. Something very bad happened to Rudy. It was going to be up to her to find Rudy and make sure he was okay. Gertie would be risking her chance of winning The Human Race to help a friend, but she knew in her heart that's what a true leader would do for a member of the team. Rudy was in trouble and Gertie was coming to the rescue!

Saturday 12:00 p.m.

Meanwhile, Yonny was still following Rudy over

mountains, through caves and around lakes, silently tagging along twenty steps behind. All Yonny could think about was how Rudy was in such great shape; he never slowed down! Yonny was breathing heavily, but Rudy was barely even breaking a sweat. Yonny knew he should have worked out prior to the race, but for some reason he just never got around to it.

Rudy was clambering quickly over a large rock when he turned half way around and said, "If you're going to follow me Yonny, you shouldn't be such a slow poke!" Yonny looked shocked. He'd been discovered!

How in the world did Rudy know he was being followed? "I'm...not...following ...you," said Yonny.

"Yeah right," exclaimed Rudy.

"How did you know," asked Yonny?

"It was simple," said Rudy. "About 10 minutes after I left you, I heard you step on a twig and it made a snapping sound. All I had to do then was listen for your heavy breathing, which by the way you should see someone about, and the rest you can probably figure out yourself."

"Are you mad at me?" asked Yonny.

"Believe it or not, no. I should be, but actually it's nice to have some company along," said Rudy. The two friends continued on at a pace that was too rapid for poor Yonny, but he wasn't about to complain—Rudy was leading the way!

Gertie, meanwhile, knew she was backtracking, but she felt it was something she had to do for a friend. She knew that her chances of becoming human were slipping away with every step backwards she took. Oh well, she thought to herself, there's always next year. What did I just say? Gertie couldn't believe her own ears... she was starting to sound like Yonny! Gertie chuckled at this realization, put her mind back on the task at hand, and continued pushing deeper and deeper back into the same dark woods from which she had emerged yesterday.

Saturday 3:00 p.m.

By this time, One Way was well ahead of the pack. His dirty tricks gained him a commanding lead, taking out many of the frontrunners. The competitors were far behind him and his only thoughts were on reaching the finish line and basking in his glorious victory. With Rudy and Yonny finally out of the way, he only saw one more potential roadblock, and her name was Gertie. If by chance he ran into her, she would be sorry!

Meanwhile, Gertie was still heading in the opposite direction of the finish line. Rumors were flying by this time and the word was getting out about her strange behavior. Every time she passed another competitor they stared at her curiously. The other road signs and traffic lights could not believe what she was doing, but sure enough, she was going in the opposite direction from the pack to save Rudy. They all knew that she was one of the favorites to win The Human Race this year. Why, they wondered, was she was throwing it all away on a domineering jerk like Rudy? It was beyond them.

Then suddenly, as if it was meant to be, Gertie ran into Ms. Yield sign.

"How's it going, Gertie?" asked Ms. Yield.

"Could be better, I guess." remarked Gertie.

"I know this may sound crazy, but I want to help you with the search for Rudy," said Ms. Yield.

"You what?" asked Gertie.

"You heard me. I want to help you rescue your friend Rudy," repeated Ms. Yield. "Believe it or not, you really know how to inspire people. I'm on board!"

Gertie was surprised at what she was hearing, and

for a moment suspected that Ms. Yield could be in cahoots with One Way. Then Gertie realized that this was a negative thought and said, "Ok, I can really use the help."

"When I said you were inspirational, I meant it," continued Ms. Yield. "I have never in my life seen Yonny act so prepared, and I know it was because of you." Ms. Yield continued. "He is like a new person. I would love to feel as confident as him. I would love to learn more about optimism from a great leader like you!"

Gertie began to blush and quickly thanked Ms. Yield for the positive feedback. She then told Ms. Yield that she was already on her way to becoming more confident, simply by having the courage to say what she had said. The two shook hands and continued on their way. As they walked along the path Gertie suddenly realized that Ms. Yield had just accomplished the secret; she understood the goal of becoming colorblind. Gertie had not discussed any information pertaining to the secret journal, but somehow, Ms. Yield grasped the concept completely. She was willing to put herself in jeopardy to help another. She was no longer looking at the other competitors as a different sign or color, but instead as friends in need of assistance.

By now, however, Rudy and Yonny were making great time and not feeling like they needed anybody's help. They finished eating lunch and were well on their way to catching up with the front-running competition. One Way was well ahead of them by this point, but it was still too early in the race to call it quits…anything could still happen!

"Where do you think Gertie is?" asked a concerned Yonny.

"Who cares?" said Rudy. "She's probably about to finish the race for all we know. She certainly isn't worried about us."

"I don't think so," said Yonny. "She really had her heart set on all of us crossing the finish line together."

"Fat chance of that happening now, we're too far behind," said Rudy.

"Never say never!" smiled Yonny.

One Way could not believe his eyes. Is that that same tree I just saw an hour ago, he thought to himself. What in the world has happened? One Way couldn't believe that he, Mr. My Way or the Highway, might possibly be lost. He was confident when he read his map yesterday that he knew exactly which route had to be taken. Now for whatever reason, he was confused. With less than twenty-four hours left in the race, this was not a good situation to be in.

Danny and his buddies sat quietly behind a pine tree and laughed as they watched One Way running around in circles. Their false trails and circular detours really paid off. Danny didn't really like to play unfair, but he also didn't care to see any participant cheat during The Human Race. He knew that One Way had in some way sabotaged the race for Rudy, and Danny didn't go for that kind of foul play. After One Way left Danny's makeshift store in the woods, Danny and his companions were certain that One Way was up to no good. It was then that they decided to beat him at his own game. They made new paths in the woods, planted fake signs, and just as they thought, One Way fell for the ruse. Danny only wished he could have done more to stop One Way from his interference in the race.

Gertie and Ms. Yield were making rapid progress backtracking to find their lost friend. As they continued to hurry along, Gertie suddenly stumbled across a huge hole in the middle of the woods. What in the world is this? She thought. As she looked into the hole she suddenly had a pretty good idea what had happened.

There, not ten feet below her in the middle of the empty hole in the middle of nowhere, she saw something that she recognized. Empty battery packages were lying on the ground. In a flash, she knew she was on the right track.

By now, One Way was furious with himself. He was losing precious time, but more importantly, he was losing the race. He was about to give up when another angry thought crossed his mind. If I can't win, no one will. He made up his mind right then and there to ruin the race for every participant possible, especially Gertie the Do-Gooder. He heard rumors that the goodie-two-shoes Gertie was back somewhere trying to help find her friends, instead of trying to win the race. He made himself a promise to find her as soon as possible and knock her out of the race for good. The only problem was, he was still lost and didn't know one way from another.

Sending Signals

Saturday 6:00 p.m.

The evening air became chilly as night began to fall. It would be dark soon. Rudy and Yonny managed to sneak onto a train that would save them at least two hours of walking. It was Yonny's idea to board the train, and Rudy begrudgingly agreed. He didn't like the idea of following someone else's suggestion, but what choice did he have- he would have been lost without Yonny's help. If he wanted to become successful and win, he had to learn to trust a little more. This was a brand new concept for Rudy, but he didn't like it one bit.

When Gertie realized that she had probably already passed Rudy during her backtracking journey to find him, she became discouraged.

"I can't believe this!" Gertie said

"I beg your pardon?" responded Ms. Yield.

"We came all this way only to find that Rudy escaped on his own. In fact, we have no clue as to where Yonny is either," said Gertie.

"Well, from the rumors we have heard from other contestants, I would venture to guess that Yonny has teamed up with Rudy," said Ms. Yield.

"Are you crazy! Rudy would never let that happen," declared Gertie.

"Let's hope for our sakes he's changed for the better after a night in the hole," said Ms. Yield.

One Way was now hot on the trail of Gertie. The rumors he was over hearing from the other racers were paying off. Without even knowing it, the other participant's were discussing Gertie's whereabouts and giving One Way perfect directions. He was closing in on her and it was only a matter of time before he captured her. He was also happy to find that Ms. Yield was helping her. Knocking two competitors out of the race was better than one.

The train that Yonny and Rudy boarded was chugging along at a rapid pace. The two decided to catch a little shut-eye before they reached their destination. Rudy fell asleep first and used his black sweatshirt for a pillow. Some good this thing has done me, Rudy thought. Yonny too fell asleep, and snored loudly as the train continued to move down the tracks swiftly.

By this time, Sammy the speed limit was well on his way to winning the race. He had a commanding lead and the excitement was growing within him. The rumors about Gertie not finishing the race because of her attempt to save Rudy were still spreading, and had reached Sammy. This both concerned Sammy and made him smile at the same time. Sammy knew that Gertie was the best leader and friend anyone could ever have. So why was he continuing to move forward, he thought to himself? Shouldn't he try to help her as well? If he turned back now, he was sure to lose the race and everything he had worked so hard for. With that thought, he suddenly stopped running. Sammy slowly turned around and faced the opposite direction from which he had just come. With a grin breaking out on his face he bent down, tightened up his running shoes and took off at a full sprint. As he started to run faster, he thought to himself, leaders like Gertie don't come around everyday. Today Sammy decided that she would be the perfect leader to follow.

Gertie and Ms. Yield apprehensively stepped onto the train. They just finished running full speed to catch the last car and were both exhausted. Gertie only hoped that she wouldn't be too late to find Rudy and Yonny before One Way had the chance to finish them off. Ms. Yield and Gertie sat down wearily and dozed for a few hours while the train rumbled on. Little did they know, that only a few cars ahead on the same train, Rudy and

Sending Signals

Yonny were doing the same thing.

One Way was sitting back in the caboose of the train just waiting for the perfect moment to attack. When he found out that Gertie and Ms. Yield sign along with Rudy and Yonny were all on the same train he couldn't believe his luck. The bribes he gave some other competitors for valuable information really paid off. Once he had all the information he needed the only logical decision was to jump on the train, get a leg up on the competition, and carry out his mission of destruction.

Sunday 12:00 a.m.

Sammy the speed limit was still running full steam ahead when he decided it was time to take a rest. He stopped at the old train station. It was the perfect place to sit and relax. Only twelve more hours and The

Human Race would be over. As Sammy contemplated the idea of becoming human he stretched out his legs and slowly drifted off to sleep. That night, Sammy dreamt of winning the race next year and in his heart he knew he would.

Ms. Yield was still sound asleep when Gertie suddenly awoke. Momentarily Gertie forgot where she was, but the soft hum of the train engine quickly reminded her. She carried the secret journal with her as she slowly walked down the dark corridors of the train in search of the kitchen. Food was the last thing on her mind, but she knew if she was to be successful in rescuing her friends, she had to stay prepared and be alert. The kitchen was closed during this time of night and the only light that could be seen was coming from the refrigerator door that appeared to be open. Someone else was looking for a midnight snack as well. Gertie quietly hid behind the stove in hopes that she would not be spotted by this late night snacker. If a human caught her in the kitchen, she would surely be finished.

The refrigerator door shut with a loud thud and then there was silence. Gertie almost screamed with delight at what she saw. Not even ten feet from where she hid, holding a taco shell stuffed with all the fixings, stood Yonny.

"Those things are better hot than cold," Gertie commented.

"Who said that?" whispered Yonny.

"Just a friend who has missed you," responded Gertie.

Instantly, Yonny knew who the voice belonged to and he dropped his taco and ran into the open arms of Gertie.

"What took you so long," laughed Yonny

"Well if you weren't so far behind in the race, I wouldn't have had to backtrack as far as I did," Gertie jokingly said.

"I knew you would come back for us," Yonny happily replied.

"What do you mean us?" asked Gertie.

"You mean to tell me that you have no idea who else is on this train?" said Yonny.

"No," replied Gertie.

"Let me put it this way, if there were pizza in this refrigerator, he would be standing here right now instead of me," Yonny said merrily.

"You mean to tell me that our good buddy Rudy is on this train right now?" Gertie asked with a smile.

"Yes, he is," said Yonny. "He and I have become quite the little team. Although, if you ask Rudy, he'll never admit it." Yonny continued to catch Gertie up on all their wild activities. He filled her in on Rudy's situation and told her about his own rescue by Danny the Detour and his friends. After he finished, he asked

Gertie if she had come alone.

"It's funny you should ask that, my little Yo-Yo friend," snickered Ms. Yield.

"What in the world are you doing here?" Yonny asked in surprise.

"She's becoming colorblind," exclaimed Gertie. "Let me explain."

Sunday 5:00 a.m.

By the time Gertie finally finished telling her story about the human named Randy and the secret journal, the sun was making its way over the horizon and the train was coming to a stop. Gertie, Yonny and Ms. Yield decided to wake up Rudy and surprise him. When they entered his room though, it was they who were surprised. Rudy was gone.

One Way was still lurking in the caboose awaiting

the arrival of the train at the station. He knew The Human Race was only a few hours from being over, and he still had to find a way to keep his enemies from winning. Although the chances were slim, there was a small possibility that Gertie, Yonny and Rudy could still pull off a victory. One Way jumped off the train before it came to a final stop and immediately began searching for his prey.

Rudy was running out of the station when he suddenly ran into Sammy the speed limit. "Out of my way, tin man!" yelled Rudy. "Where do you think you're going?" replied Sammy. "I'm going to win this race, that's where," shouted Rudy. "Don't even try to stop me." "Do you know who else is on this train?" Sammy asked cautiously.

"Who cares!" said Rudy.

"I'll tell you who cares. Your friends Gertie and Yonny, that's who."

"I know Yonny is still on the train, but you're lying about Gertie," responded Rudy.

"Am I?" said Sammy.

"Why would she be here?" asked Rudy. "I figured she would be winning the race by now."

"She would have if she wasn't such a dedicated leader," said Sammy. "She came back for you."

"Well, that's her own fault. She should have won the race when she had the chance. That's what I would have done," said Rudy. With that, he left the station.

One Way watched as all the passengers exited the train. Some of them were human and others were lights and signs. He had to find Gertie and make her pay! It was because of her positive attitude that he was in this mess in the first place. As he continued to look through the crowd, he spotted a figure running away wearing a black sweatshirt. If he couldn't catch Gertie, Rudy would have to do.

Ms. Yield sign and Yonny were discussing the colorblind issue, and how it was a fantastic idea for the two of them. Why search for the bad in others when it's so much easier to find the good. They were talking excitedly when Gertie approached.

"I can't find Rudy anywhere." Gertie sadly said. "He must have escaped once the train stopped."

"I know where he is," said Sammy, stepping out from behind a pillar.

"Holy smokes! What are you doing here?" asked a shocked Gertie.

"I'm on my way to find you!" laughed Sammy.

"What do you mean?" asked Gertie.

Sammy smiled. "It's simple. I'm here for the same reasons that Ms. Yield is here, to help you on your journey. You're a passionate leader and it's an honor to be following you."

Gertie looked up with tears in her eyes and said,

"But what about the race? There's no way you can win now."

"I've already won. Seeing how much you care for others is more rewarding than winning any race. You're a true friend who has leadership attributes that others only dream of. I'm proud to be on your team." Sammy then filled the group in on Rudy's whereabouts, as the group listened intently.

Sunday 9:00 a.m.

One Way was catching up to Rudy when he spotted Gertie and the rest of the gang out of the corner of his eye. Now he was faced with a tough decision. Should he chase Rudy and capture only one race participant, or should he capture Gertie and all her friends? After a moment's reflection, he stopped chasing Rudy and turned and started walking over toward Gertie.

Meanwhile, Rudy was running full speed ahead, and the only thought on his mind was finishing the race and becoming human. Sure, he would miss Gertie and Yonny, but the thought of becoming human was much more appealing. As Rudy continued to run, he had the strangest feeling that someone or something was following him. When he turned around to look, he found his intuition was right. Ten yards behind him was a man, a human being, gaining on him quickly.

"Stop!" yelled Randy. "You're making a big mistake."

"Get away from me, you weirdo!" screamed Rudy.

"Please, let me speak with you for just a minute," pleaded Randy. "I was once just like you." His comment stopped Rudy immediately.

"What are you talking about?" asked Rudy. "And make it quick… I have a race to win."

Randy went on to explain how he, like Rudy, once

hung from above a street corner and directed traffic. Rudy listened to his story in bewilderment. When Randy was finished, he turned toward Rudy and said, "Life is full of choices and consequences; please don't make the same wrong choice I made over 50 years ago. I once had two friends just like you, but because of my stubborn and autocratic attitude, now I can only visit them on a street corner. I became human and decided not to give them the same opportunity as me. I made a mistake that has haunted me ever since. I only hope that you don't make the same poor choice that I did."

Rudy looked up to answer, but Randy was already gone. Why should I help them? Rudy thought. Deep down, he knew the answer.

One Way was closing in on Gertie and the group and he was getting madder by the minute. His plan was to lock them inside an old semi-truck trailer that he had spotted by the train station. The only problem was how to get them there. One Way smirked when he realized he'd found the solution.

"Hey, Human Race losers!" shouted One Way.

"Stay away from us," yelled Yonny.

"I'm not going to hurt you. I've already captured the one I was looking for," said One Way.

Gertie stepped forward. "What are you talking about?"

"I have your friend Rudy tied up in the back of that old semi trailer over there," One Way pointed toward the truck and snickered. "If you want to see him alive again, I suggest you take a look for yourself."

The rear door of the old truck slid open as Gertie, Yonny, Ms. Yield and Sammy peaked inside. The truck was completely pitch dark. The group hesitantly stepped inside and began to make their way towards the back. As they journeyed further back into the truck, a loud SLAM was heard and complete darkness surrounded them. In an instant, they knew they'd been trapped by One Way and his dirty tricks.

One Way was still laughing to himself when he noticed a figure wearing a black sweatshirt sitting in one of the train cars. Oh, this is going to be easier than I thought, he imagined to himself. He quietly approached the figure with little trepidation. It's payback time for Rudy, he thought to himself as he swiftly jumped into the train car. The figure wearing the black sweatshirt didn't move. It was sitting very still. In fact, it was too still. Immediately, One Way knew something was wrong. One Way reached out and grabbed hold of the sweatshirt. The black sweatshirt was not Rudy! One Way looked down at the thing in his hands and suddenly realized that he was holding on to an old suitcase wrapped in the black sweatshirt! As he turned around to look behind him he saw the faintest glimpse of a red figure flash by. And when he heard the

SLAM, he knew he had just been tricked himself.

Rudy made a mad dash to the old semi-truck and hopped into the driver's seat. As he started the engine he chuckled to himself, Gertie always said we should take the driver's seat in life more often, I guess there is no better time than the present. The truck roared to life and Gertie, Yonny, Ms. Yield and Sammy started to slide as the truck lurched forward.

"Who's there?" shouted Gertie.

"Just your friendly neighborhood pizza delivery man," Rudy yelled back.

After driving a few miles away from the train station, Rudy let his friends out of the back of the truck and hugs were exchanged all the way around. Then the group fell silent. Emotions were running high. The Human Race was almost over, and the group was still miles away from the finish line. The chances of winning were slim.

Sending Signals

"I have an idea," said Sammy the speed limit. "I know how we can get you across the finish line in time to win." Everyone listened intently. After hearing Sammy's idea, Gertie was the first to speak up.

"If you and your family of speed limit signs try to help us, then you'll be unable to win the race yourself."

Sammy replied, "If I won without them, it would be unfair anyway. Don't worry about me. Ms. Yield and I have already discussed our plans for winning next year. This year is about you, Rudy and Yonny winning the big one. I won't take no for an answer. You three have taught me the true meaning of leadership during this race. You have led with action, not just words!"

Once they were all in agreement and Ms. Yield and Sammy said their good byes, the plan was put into immediate action. Sammy contacted his family of signs and explained his strategy of having them position themselves along the road at various spots, with their new "painted on" speed limits that helped to increase the posted speeds on the highway. All at once, new speed limit signs began appearing out of nowhere. As Rudy continued to drive along the highway, he noticed speed limit signs reading 85 mph and higher! Sammy's secret plan would allow Rudy, Yonny and Gertie to proceed to the finish line without being stopped and ticketed.

Sunday 11:45 a.m.

Just when everything was finally going good for Rudy, Yonny and Gertie a loud BANG was heard and Rudy slammed on the brakes. A flat tire was something they had not anticipated. With only a few more miles to go and only 15 minutes left, a new plan was needed.

"Oh great," complained Rudy. "Now we'll never

win."

Yonny chimed in, "Well, we gave it a good try. I guess we should probably just give up."

"Are you two serious?" said Gertie. "We did not come this far to give up just before the finish line."

"What can we do?" asked Rudy

"Yeah, we're still a good mile away from the finish line and we have no transportation," explained Yonny.

Gertie cleared her throat and spoke, "I said days ago that if we were going to win this thing, then we were going to need team work. Well, there's no better time to accomplish that then right here, right now. We all know that Rudy is the fastest out of the three of us. I'm suggesting that Rudy sprints ahead for the last mile and waits for us at the finish line. If the other competitors see him making his way to the front of the pack, they might just give up, and then Yonny and I can continue on past them. What do you think?"

"I think your crazy, that's what I think," responded Rudy. "What makes you so sure I just won't cross the finish line myself?"

"Because I trust you," said Gertie.

"Me too," said Yonny.

"Why do you trust me all of a sudden?" wondered Rudy.

Gertie winked at Rudy and said, "It's not all of a sudden. I've always trusted you. That's part of leadership. Leaders are most effective when the people they are leading do the 'right thing' even when the leader is not present. I believe you'll do the right thing, Rudy. In fact, I know it!"

Sunday 11:57 a.m.

One by one, the other participants in The Human Race stopped running and moved to the side to let

Rudy pass. Rudy could not believe his eyes. These competitors were actually choosing to step aside and let him take the lead. The finish line was in his sights. The crowd that had gathered around was cheering him on. All around you could hear "Rudy-Rudy-Rudy." Only a few more steps and he would be there! The defining moment he had waited for so long was finally here. But the real defining moment in Rudy's life came when he approached the finish line and stopped just shy of crossing. He was faced with a decision. One more step and he would be human. The race would be over. He could plunge on ahead alone, or wait for his friends to catch up. As he thought about this, he looked up at the bright blue sky and the sun shining down on him and realized he was part of something greater than himself: a team.

When Yonny and Gertie reached the finish line, Rudy could not tell them apart. Their individual colors of yellow and green seemed to be the same. When he looked down at himself, he could not decipher his own coloring either. At first, Rudy thought his eyes were seeing things, because he had been staring into the sun for such a long time, but in the end he knew the truth. He had become colorblind!

With hands clasped tightly, the three individual lights crossed the finish line as one.

PART FOUR
THE NEXT DAY

PART FOUR
THE NEXT DAY

Monday 7:00 a.m.

Rudy, Yonny, and Gertie woke up bright and early the next morning. They were exhausted from the past three days and all they wanted to do was sleep in. Just as Yonny was about to hit the snooze button for the second time, he realized he was alone. Slowly and cautiously he crept out of bed. Where am I, he wondered? Where are Rudy and Gertie? Where is the old metal casing that used to be my home? Why do my legs look longer and my arms feel stronger? Why is there a little league baseball coach's uniform on my dresser? He slowly turned the shirt around and across the back he read "Yonny Lightning, Head Coach." Was he dreaming, or was this what he thought it was?

Sending Signals

Meanwhile, 30 miles away our little friend Gertie was making her way to the office to start her workday. As she was driving down the freeway, she suddenly slammed on the brakes and pulled the car over to the side of the road. It can't be, she thought. I must be dreaming! I don't even own a car let alone know how to drive one. She noticed something hanging around her rearview mirror that appeared to be a name badge. When she glanced up to read the name she almost fell over! "Gertie Lightning, Vice President." How could she be the V.P. of a company when she was only a little traffic light? It was at that moment a little light bulb flashed in her mind: The Human Race! She looked around for Rudy and Yonny, but they were nowhere to be found. Could it really be true? Could she really be a human? As she closed her eyes with a great big smile stretching across her face from ear to ear, she knew the answer was Yes.

The loud blaring siren woke Rudy up from his sound sleep. He quickly put on his fireman's uniform and slid down a steel metal pole. Without hesitation he grabbed his best flashlight and ran through the station. Where was he? Why was he getting dressed in a fireman's uniform? Why was he, along with four other people rushing around the station, getting ready to board a big red fire engine? When he put on his jacket, he suddenly noticed a name stitched into it that read "Rudy Lightning, Volunteer Fireman." As he and his team pulled out of the fire station, he realized that something magical had happened. Because of his leadership ability and the cooperation of his two friends Yonny and Gertie, he was really human!

As the fire engine raced down the street, he thought to himself again and again... I guess teamwork really does pay off.

The baseball field was packed with hundreds of

excited fans and players anxiously awaiting the start of the final game of the season. Yonny's team was undefeated, and they were getting ready to play the biggest game of their lives. If the team won, they would be the little league champions of the 10-and-under division. What an accomplishment that would be. While Yonny was proudly leading his team onto the field for batting practice, he noticed his two assistant coaches bickering back and forth.

"I think the line up should be this way!" screamed Jim.

"You're wrong and you know it!" yelled Bob. Yonny quickly and assertively stepped in between the two, and asked if he could help solve the problem.

Yonny listened to both sides of the argument without passing any judgment. He understood both coaches and knew why they were upset. He started to tell the coaches that they reminded him of his old friends Rudy and Gertie, but he thought it best if he didn't go around mentioning that he used to be a traffic light. What would Gertie do if she were here, he wondered? Be The Driver came to mind! At that moment Yonny realized that he was going to be the one to settle this debate. A leader was needed and he was ready for the job. It was time to put his Yo-Yo thoughts away and become the leader he knew he could be. Although he still appreciated his "think things through" mentality, he realized there were a time and a place for everything. This was the time to lead, not follow. This was definitely a new Yonny.

As Gertie pulled into the parking lot, she noticed a parking space with her name on it. She cautiously pulled in and shut the car engine off. She got out and looked up at the enormous 20-story building where she worked and suddenly became nervous. Did she really have what it took to be a supervisor? As a traffic light, she was bold and optimistic, but as a human being, she wasn't so sure. After a few minutes of positive self-encouragement, she confidently walked into her new building. She noticed a receptionist and asked her if she was heading in the right direction. The receptionist looked confused, but pointed her the right way. After about five minutes of aimlessly walking about, Gertie finally found her office. She opened the door and made herself at home. Everything she had always hoped for was coming true.

After an hour of going through some paper work, she noticed in her daily planner that a meeting was scheduled for that morning. Wow, she thought, my first meeting as a human. She looked at the clock on the wall and realized that it started in five minutes! She quickly gathered her brief case and headed out of her office. When she opened the door of the conference room, 15 human faces were looking up at her. This was her moment to shine!

The big red fire engine continued to race down the street with its siren blaring. The lessons Rudy learned during The Human Race were still fresh in his mind, and he decided he would apply them to his current situation. He was part of a team, and that made him (surprisingly) feel comfortable. If only Gertie and Yonny could see me now, he thought to himself.

The fire engine screeched to a stop and the firemen quickly rushed to the burning house. With no time to think they instinctively went to work. Rudy, with flashlight in hand, entered the house first. There was black smoke everywhere and his keen visual perception was gone. He heard a scream from above and quickly headed for the steps. Because of his blurred vision, he had to feel his way around. He was having a difficult time finding the steps on his own, so he decided to ask his fellow workers for help. One firefighter in the group suggested that they create a "human chain."

Sending Signals

Each firefighter was to lock arms with another ahead and behind, and this would give Rudy the chance to climb the stairs and still know which way was which. It wasn't Rudy's idea, but he agreed to it anyway.

As he approached the second floor he heard the screaming again. This time he knew from which room the noise was coming. Rudy and the human chain crept forward, slowly moving towards the sound. Rudy kicked in the door and instantly felt the back draft of the fire. The force of the pressure built up inside the room knocked him to the floor. For a moment, he thought he was done for. Then from out of nowhere, his team reappeared by his side, and he was up on his feet in no time at all. He noted in the back of his mind that he would have to thank his co-workers later for their much-needed help. Without hesitation, he led the team back into the room and rescued the stranded little boy who was screaming for help.

When everyone was out of the house and the area was secure, Rudy thanked his entire team and told them that he admired their leadership ability and quick thinking. He approached the firefighter who had the idea of the human chain and thanked him personally. "Because of your leadership ability, I'm alive right now," said Rudy. "I always thought that my leadership ideas were best, but today you proved me wrong. Thank You!"

On the way back to the station, Rudy pondered this new idea of there being many different styles of leadership. In the past, he had always believed that his way was best. Although his leadership style was effective at times, he was now able to look at other types of leadership with admiration. The human chain idea had saved the day, and he knew in his heart that he would have never thought of it. Letting another leader share a great idea was the best lesson he could have learned. As he sat on the back of the truck on the way back to the station, he closed his eyes and privately thanked Yonny and Gertie.

The two coaches, with the help and guidance of Yonny, worked out their differences. Yonny showed excellent leadership ability in dealing with the problem at hand. As head coach, it was his responsibility to manage and lead the team. And as he ran out on the field with his team he realized that managing individual people is what allows a team to run smoothly. As his little league team prepared for the final game of the season, Yonny realized it really didn't matter if they won or lost; instead, it was the experience and insights they had gained along the way to the season finale, and the way they'd responded eagerly to his leadership.

The conference room was large and rectangular with full-length picture windows everywhere. As the sunlight gleamed through, it cast a bright beam of light on the 15 faces awaiting the arrival of their trusty Vice President. Gertie slowly made her way to the only available seat—the one that was located at the head of the table. The first thing she did surprised her fellow colleagues. She told everyone to get up and move down three chairs. At first they just starred at her as if she were joking, but soon they realized that she was serious. One by one, they each got up and moved down three chairs, all the while smiling and laughing. "That's just what this conference room needs, a little more laughter," said Gertie. "If we're going to be making million dollar decisions, we should at least feel relaxed." The group eased back into their chairs and the meeting continued. The minutes were read and the new agenda ideas were presented.

After the meeting was adjourned, the president of the company approached Gertie and said, "Now I know why I pay you the big bucks." They both laughed and walked out of the conference room together.

Sending Signals

Gertie returned to her office and was surprised to find one of her employees waiting for her. Ben had been with the company for nearly 17 years, and in that time climbed up the corporate ladder very successfully. He started out in the mailroom and gradually moved his way up to a manager's position. He was well respected and liked by everyone. Today, however, something was bothering him.

"Hi Gertie, I hope you don't mind me dropping in like this?"

"Of course not Ben, that's why I'm here. What can we do for you?"

Her response confused him. She was the only person in the room besides him, what did she mean by we? He looked up and said, "I'm sorry, I don't understand. Who's we?"

"It's simple," exclaimed Gertie. "Whatever your situation is, it needs to be reviewed by both of us, not just me. If I tell you what to do, then you have just become a passenger. I will give you all the advice I can, but I want to include you every step of the way." This style of leadership was definitely new to Ben. He explained to Gertie how in the past, all supervisor problems had been handled by the V.P. He went on to mention that the old V.P. always did things his way.

Gertie just smiled and said, "I wonder why he isn't working here any more!" Ben smiled back and understood exactly what she meant by that remark. At that moment, Gertie thought of her old friends Rudy and Yonny, and wondered what they might be up to.

The fire engine slowly backed into the station and assumed its "ready" position in the firehouse. After Rudy and his co-workers washed the truck and hit the showers, they all met up in the kitchen. "That was some fire," said one of his colleagues.

"Tell me about it," said Rudy, "I almost didn't make

it back here today. It's a good thing I have friends like you at my side." And just at that moment, he remembered his old friends and wondered how Yonny and Gertie were managing in the real world.

With runners on second and third base, the game was looking like it might go into extra innings. Yonny's team was up three runs, but the opposing team had their best hitter at the plate. This slugger was known for his home runs late in the game. If he got a hold of one, it would tie the game. It was a full count and the pitcher was looking nervous. Suddenly Yonny called a time out.

The two assistant coaches were making their way out to the mound when Yonny heard a voice from deep within the back of his mind say "Be the Driver." The assistant coaches were always the ones who made the decisions during crunch time. When they were half way there, Yonny called for them to stop. They walked back to the dug out and Yonny said, "I think I should be the one to speak with our pitcher."

The one assistant coach said, "Do you think or do you know?"

"I know," Yonny said more confidently. "But before I go out there, I would like to hear your input as well." The two assistant coaches gave their advice, and Yonny nodded and proceeded out to the pitcher's mound.

The young pitcher was surprised to see Yonny appear at the mound. "Hey coach, what took you so long?"

"A lifetime of fear, I guess," said Yonny. The young boy smiled and anxiously waited to hear Yonny's advice. Yonny asked the boy what his favorite pitch was and the boy replied, "Fastball." Yonny knew the consequences of what could happen if the batter hit the fastball. "What's your second favorite pitch?" asked Yonny. "Curveball," said the little boy. Yonny knew that the batter was probably waiting for a curveball, though, so he told his young pitcher to throw the fastball. The young boy looked at him and said, "Are you sure?"

"I've never been so sure in all my life," came the reply from Yonny.

Yonny walked back to the dugout and never looked back. The pitcher took a deep breath and began his wind up. The fans in the stands stood motionless as the ball was released from the pitcher's hand. "STRIKE THREE!" yelled the umpire. The crowd went wild! The dugout erupted with applause, and Yonny sat back and reveled in the big win at season's end. As he shut his eyes, he thought of his two friends Rudy and Gertie, and wondered if they were having as much fun as he was.

Two weeks had gone by since Rudy, Yonny, and Gertie had become human. Rudy was still busy fighting fires, while Yonny continued to bask in his victory. Gertie was really changing things around for her company, as sales steadily increased by 20 percent. The real world was treating everyone just fine.

It was Saturday afternoon when Rudy boarded the bus and asked the driver if he would make a special stop. The driver said yes, and the bus moved out. Meanwhile, Gertie was just leaving the grocery store when she abruptly decided to take an alternate route home. About the same time, Yonny was jogging around his neighborhood when he suddenly felt the strong urge to extend his jog. He wasn't going home, in fact he was heading in the opposite direction.

The bus pulled up to a stop and Rudy hesitantly stepped down. He walked to the nearest gas station and got himself a soda. The scenery at the old intersection was just as he remembered. The corner of Hansen and Heart was looking as busy as ever.

Gertie found a spot on the street and parked her car.

Sending Signals

She glanced around the area as she fed two quarters into the meter. She couldn't believe it had been two weeks since she seemed like a permanent fixture on the corner where she now stood. Hansen and Heart had never looked better.

Yonny slowed his pace down while he waited for the "walk" light to illuminate. Five blocks away was a place very familiar to him. Should he continue on or turn back? He knew where turning back would take him, but what about what lay ahead? Then he remembered something he had heard a long time ago: Opportunities exist...if you go looking for them! With that in mind, he picked up his pace again and continued his jog. Two blocks further down, he passed the local taco stand and smiled. No time for tacos today, he thought. Today was a chance for opportunity! What that opportunity was, he did not know, but as he approached his old stomping grounds of Hansen and Heart, he thought he had a pretty good idea.

"Good morning, losers!" laughed Rudy.

"Good morning stubborn boy," exclaimed Gertie.

"Yo-Yo here, at your service," giggled Yonny. The three friends stared at each other for what seemed like a lifetime, and then immediately embraced in a hug that warmed their souls and filled their hearts. They did not let go for some time, and when they did finally let go, they hugged each other again! The chance of all three meeting at the same time on the same day was incredibly remote. Some might say it was fate, some may say it was luck, but the three of them knew it was actually teamwork!

Rudy filled his friends in about his new life as a fireman and about his recent encounter with danger on the job. He promised to take them on a tour of the fire station and even let them sound the siren. Yonny explained about his leadership role on the baseball field. He mentioned his team's championship victory, and Rudy and Gertie said they would definitely go to some of his games next season. Gertie told them about her new position as V.P. and how she was enjoying the challenge. "Management is about leading people," she said, "not organizations." All three unanimously agreed that the lessons they had learned while running The Human Race had helped them effectively prepare for life in the real world.

After a few hours of catching up with one another, they agreed to meet once a week for lunch at the corner of Hansen and Heart. They decided that each friend would have the opportunity to "lead" the others to where they would like to eat. Deep down they all knew that pizza, donuts, and tacos would still be on their menu of choice.

When it was finally time for them to say their good byes, they all agreed that one more thing had to be done.

Rudy, Yonny and Gertie walked into the middle of the street at the corner of Hansen and Heart and looked up. A light breeze rustled the air as they stood looking up in amazement. Above them, which now seemed like a million miles away, stood their replacement. The new little traffic light was shiny and bright. It swayed back and forth, but did not make a sound. Rudy, Yonny and Gertie each wondered if they were being watched as they stood below on the street. Without a doubt, they knew the answer was yes.

They each went home a separate way that day, but before they were out of hearing distance from each other, there came a parting call from their three different directions: "GOOD LUCK!"

PART FIVE
TODAY

PART FIVE
TODAY

The Human Race is a race that continues to this day, and it has become part of our everyday lives in ways that you might not notice. Whether you're a supervisor or a stay-at-home parent, the challenges and opportunities for leadership moments come up with surprising regularity. Deciding where to eat lunch, or picking out a video from the movie store, can be a leadership opportunity. Collaborating, cooperating and taking charge in times of crisis—these are leadership challenges. Leadership means exerting the right kind of influence, direction and assistance. On a daily basis, often without thinking about it, we try to influence a great number of people. The question we have to ask ourselves is, do we lead like Rudy, like Yonny or like Gertie?

Sending Signals

Each style of leadership has its pros and cons. The good news is that we all have a little bit of each style within ourselves. The Rudy style of leadership means that the job will most likely get done, but it may require an aggressive attitude toward others. This type of leadership can cause a person to appear mean and stubborn. If there were a war being fought, however, this would be the leadership style most people would like to see demonstrated from their Generals. In this situation, the commanding officer should not vacillate and appear wishy-washy when making a life or death decision.

The Yonny style of leadership is passive and has that old "think things through" mentality. If you were lying on an operating table, undergoing a risky procedure, this type of leadership might be very desirable in your doctor. The careful, reflective surgeon would think things through, and then proceed with the safest approach possible. In the same situation, a Rudy-style leader might make a hasty decision without proper planning, not bothering to ask anyone else's opinion. Operating room staff have to work as a team- surgeon, cardiologist, anesthesiologist, lead nurse, scrub tech- and each member of the group has important skills and knowledge to contribute.

The Gertie style of leadership is assertive, but this type of leadership has the valuable ability to be flexible. Gertie leaders can make decisions on their own if they have to, but more often they like to have input from other members of the team. When a leader such as this is in charge, others feel like their opinions are valued and considered. Although individual ideas or inputs might not be chosen, the group still has a role in the overall decision-making process. A Gertie leader typically has a loyal following because they want to, not because they have to. This type of leader is very positive.

When it comes to leading people, you always have to use your best judgment about what works best. No one style of leadership is perfectly suited to every situation. If a quick decision needs to be made, let your Rudy make it. If you have some time to think over a decision, let your Yonny get involved. When you're making a decision that requires multiple theories, inputs and opinions, be a Gertie type of leader and draw upon the insights of others. In the end, leadership is a lot like the larger game of life. When faced with leadership situations, you really have only two choices: be the leader or be the follower. Or to put it another way, be the driver or be the passenger. In general, being the driver is much more productive and rewarding!

So remember, the next time you see a traffic light that appears to be "out of order," think again. That light might be sending you a signal telling you to take charge of your life, become a leader and empower others by your own example. Instead of assuming that those signals are automatic and inhuman, look up and say hello, because you never know who might be watching you!

THE END

Brian Blasko is a highly motivated professional speaker, trainer, author and consultant. His seminars and workshops are specifically designed to inspire individual and organizational growth.

Brian has inspired the youngest of scholars and the most seasoned business professionals to feel comfortable about themselves. His philosophies enable everyone to discover, maximize and succeed not only in business, but in their personal environments as well.

Blasko is to motivation... as engine is to car. He has an M.A. in interpersonal communication, is a distinguished member of the National Speakers Association and for the past decade has consulted with and conducted seminars and workshops for numerous local, national and international organizations. Brian, his lovely wife Laura and their three children, Benjamin, Angelee and Natalie reside in Youngstown, Ohio.

Let Brian **turbo charge** *your next event with one of his inspirational...*

high octane *programs!*

www.BrianBlasko.com